The Dreamwork Book

A Guide to Remembering and Interpreting Your Dreams

Zoilita Grant, MS, CHT

ISBN 1-890575-01-1

Published in the United States in 1997 by

MasterKey, Inc.

P. O. Box 17474, Boulder, CO 80308

303/ 939-8907 Fax: 303/ 682-2384

Email: masterkey@selfhealing.com

Website: www.selfhealing.com

TABLE OF CONTENTS

Chapter 1
Dreams and History

Throughout recorded history, dreams have made up an important part of people's lives. Stories of precognitive and lucid dreams abound in both the Old and New Testaments. Ancient cultures throughout the world reflect a rich and varied world of dreams that influenced political decisions, marriages, inventions, writers, artists, scientists, prophets and saints.

Alexander the Great, who was on the verge of giving up his siege of Tyre, dreamed one night of a dancing satyr. Aristander, Alexander's dream interpreter, figured out the dream by splitting the word "Satyros" into two words, "sa Turos"—Greek for "thine is Tyre." Alexander went on to attack and conquer Tyre.

Robert Louis Stevenson (1850-1894) had a vivid and extremely active dream life. He was tormented by nightmares as a child, and as an adult he entertained himself nightly with fascinating dreams. This change appears to have come about as he gained control over his dreams. Stevenson claimed that many of his stories were given to him "in bits and pieces" while dreaming.

Joseph, in the New Testament, was told of the pregnancy of Mary. He was also warned of Herod's plan to kill the child Jesus. After the death of Herod, an angel appeared in a dream and told Joseph that he and his family could return to the land of Israel.

To the Senoi people, who reside in the mountainous jungles of Malaysia, dreams are an integral part of everyday life. Senoi families discuss their dreams at breakfast every morning and a large part of their day is spent pursuing dream-depicted activities; children make artistic or mechanical things seen in their dreams, others create costumes, paintings or perform dream-inspired dances. Tribe members even agree on when to move their village based on dream discussions. Although it is not known what effect the dream world has on psychological adjustment, it is a fact that neuroses and psychoses among the Senoi people are nonexistent.

Though there are still cultures today that recognize the importance of dreams, for most of us dreams are just insignificant manifestations that occur when we sleep. Unless our dreams are notable, as many nightmares tend to be, few of us can even recall the dreams we do have.

Sigmund Freud, in his study *The Interpretation of Dreams*, held forth that all dreams stem from unacceptable, hidden wishes and fears. Dreams were reduced to an expression of repressed instinctive wishes. Much emphasis was put on memories of infant sexuality, resulting in a complex and often tangled interpretation of dreams. Although Freud never succeeded in linking his psychological theories with neurobiological ones, he went on to create one of the most complex dream theories ever put forth.

Karl Jung believed that the symbols often encountered in dreams provided a bridge for greater clarity between our waking lives and our personal mythologies. Dreams allowed the unconscious to reveal our talents and desires. They show us the instinctual pattern by which our lives will unfold. In this sense, dreams are our personal oracles.

Early psychologists tried to find, in the normal process of dreaming, a key to understanding the abnormal mental states of mental illness. Because dreaming is like hallucinating, with vivid images which are similar to the visions psychotics experienced, most of the early research is seen from this perspective.

In 1977, Robert W. McCarley and J. Allen Hobson, two Harvard University scientists, developed a theory that contradicted Freud's views. They proposed that biological processes in the brain can completely explain the content of dreams. Thus, there is no need for any psychological explanation of dream content. They maintain that the brain stem's stimulation of the cortex during the dream state occurs in a chance manner. The cortex, attempting to make sense of this random stimulation, brings forth the confused images and bizarre story plots that make up most dreams. This theory has been widely criticized and most psychologists still consider dreams to be psychologically important.

One should keep in mind that most scientists have always looked upon dream interpretation as something less than an exact science. So little is really understood about the workings of our brains, that what we do know often doesn't fit into one of those little categories that science depends so much upon. An individual's dreams can be personal, intimate, and so intertwined with their own belief systems, that few, if any, scientific theories can account for their meaning.

Although many of the early dream theories have been discarded in recent years, the interpretation of dreams among psychologists continues to this day. With dozens of dream theories to draw from, we need not fear the demise of dream interpretation in the near future.

Chapter 2
The Importance of Dreaming

S ince REM sleep was discovered in 1953, there have been numerous theories put forth concerning dreams– what causes dreams, the need for dreams, the importance of dreams, etc. The speculation and study continues to the present; however, there are a few definite things we know about the dream world. All members of the mammal kingdom experience REM sleep. REM is described as rapid eye movement, in which both eyes move quickly and alertly in unison, as though the sleeper were watching something from beneath trembling eyelids. REM sleep time occurs in the first stage of sleep and occupies from 20 to 25 per cent of a normal adult's sleeping time and over 50 per cent of a baby's sleeping time. Thus, we spend about two hours a night dreaming. The amount of REM sleep cannot be increased by manipulating external circumstances. This means that dreaming is more connected to subjective than objective reality.

Although most adults remember few of their dreams, *all of us dream nightly*. People deprived of REM sleep exhibit signs of severe mental psychosis within 36 to 48 hours. People have been known to develop psychotic hallucinations and delusions.

REM sleep benefits our entire mental functioning. I recently saw a Star Trek episode in which the crew was not allowed to have dreams—the result was that everyone's brain started to deteriorate. That is actually what *would* happen to us if we didn't dream. REM sleep provides rest and recovery periods for the part of the brain that regulates attention, memory and mood. During this period, our memories are updated as we integrate new experiences into our memory banks in an emotionally relevant way.

The average adult dreams from three to five times during eight hours of sleep. The dreams occur roughly every 90 to 100 minutes and last from 5 to 30 minutes each. During the dream state, the pathways that carry nerve impulses from the brain to the muscles are blocked. Therefore, the body cannot move while in a dream state. At the same time, the cerebral cortex—the part of the brain involved in higher functions—is extremely active. It is known that the cortex is stimulated by neurons that carry impulses from the brain stem.

We continue to sleep during the REM period, despite the fact that our brains are highly active, because both our sensory input and motor output are blocked. The muscles, nerve fibers and neurons in the spinal cord are inhibited, protecting our bodies from physical harm during the dream state. Sleepwalking or talking in one's sleep seldom occurs during REM sleep.

There is a lot of emotional content in our dreams. Unresolved conflicts, concerns about performance, and feelings about people and situations are played out in the dream world. Dreaming seems to provide a means of releasing tension and anxieties that we unconsciously suppress during our waking lives.

The Importance of Dreaming

It is interesting to note that many terminal cancer patients cannot remember their dreams. Since cancer is often linked to repression of feelings, it seems that even the dream's information is repressed. It is much healthier to express the content of the dreams rather than to repress them. In the process of becoming whole, dreams of violence, murder, even death, are all ways in which our subconscious is allowing a milieu of thoughts, feelings and impressions to escape our busy minds. Dreams give us *release* from our inner conflicts and *insight* into our personal potential and promise.

Dreaming is a process and the dream is a creation produced by our minds to create harmony in our lives.

During our waking life we are always receiving clues and insights from our Inner Self, but we are usually too busy to pay attention. We are too busy, too distracted–too caught in our lives– to hear important messages that come from inside. In our conscious waking life we are not always open to the messages. We may also be unwilling to look at what is really happening with our lives. It is during the dream state that this information is often revealed.

Dreams are also direct routes into our Higher Consciousness/ Inner Selves. **Dreams may contain the most direct spiritual teaching we can receive.**

Dreams serve many functions which support our waking lives: they allow the brain to sort and file data that has been acquired during the day; they allow the mind to release any emotional tension that has not been processed during the day; they are doorways to the subconscious and help us to see how we really feel about our lives. Our dreams tell us the truth about ourselves. They are an expression of our sense of ourself.

BRAIN FUNCTIONS

Left Hemisphere	**Right Hemisphere**
Dominates the right side of the body	Dominates the left side of the body
Temporal relationships	Spatial relations
Linear time sense	Simultaneousness

Thinking:
    analytical
    logical
    abstract
    sequential
    cause & effect
	Thinking:
	    synthetic
	    imaginative
	    holistic
	    a-causal
	    metaphorical

Speech	Art:
	    music (untrained)
	    drawing

Grammar	depth perception
	    complex visual patterns
	    recognition of faces

Naming	gestures & facial expression
	    gestalts
	    shapes, colors, textures,

Math	forms
Music	Dreaming ESP Meditation / Hypnosis
Logician, critic, analyst	**Artist, inventor, innovator**

The Importance of Dreaming

Every dream you have relates directly to some facet of your life. In one sense the dream world is as real as waking reality—not objectively so, like a chair, but it is as real as our waking life in the sense that it contains real teaching lessons for our lives.

It is so very beneficial to work with our dreams. Our divine personal guidance comes through loud and clear because we are not consciously editing the information. It comes through whether we like it or not, whether we invite it or not.

It is important to remember our being is more than just a physical body. Our being contains our spiritual self—our truth, our souls. Our dream world can frequently reveal this to us better than our waking life. Our lives contain lessons for our souls and in some senses the dream world provides learning experiences that more directly involve our souls.

Dreams are essential for our salvation. Salvation comes from the Greek word salvos—meaning wholeness, health. It has a lot to do with the integration of the various aspects of ourselves. Sometimes these parts are cut off from our objective consciousness. By making the separate parts of ourselves one, dreams become an essential step in the process of our becoming a whole, healthy person.

Why is it that most of us fail to remember a single dream? The reasons for this failure to recall our dreams varies from one individual to the next; however, there are five reasons that are very common.

1. Since dreams occur all night, the time period between our dream and when we wake up may be too long, resulting in our not remembering the dream.

2. We suppress, or choose not to remember the information we receive—it might challenge our cherished belief system, or we may interpret the information as threatening.

3. There is a shift in awareness or consciousness that takes place when we move from the dreaming state to the waking state, making it difficult to retain information from one state of consciousness to another. Therefore, what we learn in an altered state of consciousness will be remembered best when back in that particular altered state. It is the shift in consciousness which also makes it hard to retain the information. The brain wave patterns are different in the dream state than in waking consciousness.

4. We do not value our dreams—our subconscious knows this and doesn't retain the information. This is primarily a cultural factor. Throughout recorded history, humankind has valued dreams and found them to be a source of guidance, inspiration, prophecy and problem solving. The Egyptians, Babylonians, Greeks and Romans all believed dreams to be an important way in which the soul received guidance from the spiritual world. Native American Indians believed that visions and dreams would come from the Great Spirit to guide the soul. Without this guidance, man's lower nature–which inclines to ignorance, cruelty and apathy–would prevail. The soul enlightened by dreams can achieve the nobility for which humanity was created. The Bible also mentions the importance of dreams. Ancient people's beliefs in dreams gave them a connection to the sources of spiritual life, but our culture is greatly impoverished in this respect and there is a wide gulf between our conscious life and the life of our souls.

5. We don't have the *intention* to remember our dreams. When we consciously want to remember our dreams we have a better chance of doing so. Our minds respond to motivation and intention.

This book will teach you to program yourself to remember your dreams and will give you the skills necessary to do specific work with your dreams. You will be using your sleeping time in a constructive way to affect your life.

Dreams are a common experience to all of us—everyone dreams! **When we work with our dreams, we can make profound changes in our waking lives.**

Chapter 3
Remembering your Dreams

The first thing to do in any dream program is to learn how to *remember* your dreams. Everyone can learn to do this, and it is an essential step in using your dreams in a more productive way.

You must begin to develop the habits of remembering and recording your dreams. By creating the *intent* to remember them, you set in motion the process that will allow you to do so.

Every night before you go to bed, tell yourself to remember and record your dreams. I highly recommend the Dreamwork tape that was developed to accompany this book. The Dreamwork tape is designed to help you have dreams which are clear, helpful and relevant to your waking life. This tape takes you through the process of programming your subconscious to create dreams to work on your issues. It also helps you to remember and understand your dreams.

If you do not have the tape, simply relax your mind and body. Tell yourself: "My dreams are clear, concise, and helpful. I will remember my dreams and write them down in the morning."

The very suggestion that your dreams can be of practical help starts the process enabling you to remember them. Being motivated to recall your dreams improves your ability to do so. It is the same mechanism that helps us wake up at a certain time when we really need to. You can even use language to support your recall, such as saying, "I remember a dream I had last night," rather than, "I had a dream last night."

Expect to remember and write down a dream as soon as you open your eyes. Keep your Dreamwork Book and some writing materials close to your bedside. Writing down your dreams, or journaling, is as important as remembering the individual dream. It allows you to see the patterns that are developing in your subconscious. Since our dreams work on numerous levels, it is helpful to have enough writing space to take a look at many different levels. When you do the dreamwork, start with your physical world and move towards the spiritual.

Journaling can become a very important part of your life. You can do more than write down your dreams—you can include a list of your current activities, things you need to buy, prayer lists, and goals you want to accomplish. Keeping all these together allows you to write down guidance, intuitive insights, and information from your Inner Self as they relate to your life. Consistent dreamwork also aids in further developing the right hemisphere of your brain. Refer back to page 8 to see what brain functions will be improved.

Since dreams take place in another state of consciousness, it is often difficult to retain their content. It is important to write down as much as you can about the dream as soon as you wake up. Be sure to record any impressions, images, or dialogue connected with the dream. If you cannot remember the content, focus instead on any *feelings* that you have upon awakening. The more details you can remember, the easier it will be to ascertain the dream's meaning.

If you don't like to write, you can draw or paint your dream. This can be equally powerful and will allow for a great deal of insight.

As you work with your dreams you will be building bridges between different levels of consciousness, increasing your ability to learn from your dreams. Since this process will also greatly develop the right hemisphere of the brain, you will begin to have a much strong connection to your intuition ... your Inner Self.

GENERAL STRATEGIES FOR
REMEMBERING DREAMS

- Go to bed early. Don't let yourself get overtired before going to sleep.

- Review and process your day before going to sleep.

- Tell yourself (or use the Dreamwork tape) to remember your dreams.

- Keep the Dreamwork Book and writing materials close by.

- Stay in bed an extra few minutes reviewing your dreams.

- Relive the dream. (Alchemy technique - see pg. 36 for definition)

- Record everything you remember, including how you felt.

- Discuss your dreams with someone else. You may find that by relating your dream, you release new information that you hadn't noticed before.

- Use the Dream Techniques (Chapter 7) to work on your dreams.

Chapter 4
Types of Dreams

reams can be divided into five types and as you get more comfortable with dream work, you will be able to discern them. Each type of dream has different implications for your life. These dreams are *clearing, interference, teaching, issue solving,* and *spiritual.*

CLEARING DREAMS

Clearing dreams assist you in processing and resolving personal experiences of the day. They allow you to sort through all the emotional and mental reactions in your life. Through this process you remove the clutter and rerun every experience as you need to. These types of dreams serve to release pressure, stress, anxiety and other emotions you may have retained. They also help the body and mind to relax. If you consciously clear the mind and relax the body before you go to sleep, you can eliminate the need for these types of dreams. This clearing can be done through meditation before you sleep or by rerunning the day's events in your mind—releasing and processing.

INTERFERENCE DREAMS

These dreams are created by circumstances that are happening in the outside world. Loud noises and distinct smells can be incorporated into these dreams and may not be accurate symbols for interpretation. Sometimes a television program playing in another room can affect the content of the dream. So it is important to be aware of these factors before you begin to try to understand your dreams. The condition of your body—aches and pains, as well as the contents of your stomach can also affect your dreams. It is important to try to sleep in a quiet and peaceful place to get the most accurate meaning of your dreams.

TEACHING DREAMS

Teaching dreams can give you important information about problems you are facing. You ordinarily have one teaching dream a night. These dreams help you prepare for things that are happening right now in your life. Sometimes in teaching dreams you will find yourself in a classroom, a school, or with a teacher. These dreams may present alternative ways in which you might deal with situations and relationships. Intuitive insights, creative ideas, especially prevalent in the world of literature, and many scientific discoveries were initiated through these types of dreams.

ISSUE SOLVING DREAMS

It is possible to specifically program your dreams to solve the issues in your waking life. You can gain insights and understanding about issues in your life once you learn how to program your dreams. It is also possible to understand relationships or get help with career choices through the dream world.

Types of Dreams

Your dreams are an incredibly valuable resource in your life. It is important to learn how to remember, understand and program your dreams.

SPIRITUAL DREAMS

Under spiritual dreams, we have dreams of the future and dreams that are messages from our Inner Self/ Higher Power/God. Both of these types of dreams have a similar quality which is very different from all the other types of dreams. Dreams that give us glimpses of the future come from an intuitive level. The more that you work with them, the more accurate your intuitive senses will become. Dreams that show the future are called precognitive. These dreams and message dreams are usually tied up with your spiritual growth. They may either be focused on some spiritual truth or may be personal messages for your life. The more spiritual your dreams become, the greater the possibility to get divine guidance for your life. These types of dreams are intended to direct the attention inward and increase your knowledge of your Spiritual Self.

Chapter 5

UNDERSTANDING YOUR DREAMS

We have already learned that dreams are produced in a state of consciousness which is different from our waking state. That fact alone makes it difficult to understand them. You are never going to understand the real meaning of dreams from a rational point of view. Learning to work with dreams may seem very awkward at first but as you practice, it will get easier. Like playing the guitar or working on a computer, practice will improve your ability to understand and comprehend what your dreams mean.

There is a lot more going on in the dream state than we realize. There are many levels in the dream world. Just remembering dreams is helpful—it aids in integrating parts of ourselves which we have walled off. It takes a lot of energy to keep these parts separate—and there is a release of energy just through dreaming it. As we work with our dreams we move more and more into an area called *lucid dreaming* where we actually know that we are dreaming when we are dreaming. Allowing yourself free rein during the dream state helps to bring a state of mental balance.

Dreams can't be analyzed. They must be systematized, experienced, and integrated into our lives. Dreams come from the right hemisphere of our brain. Dreams allow us to release energy and balance our lives. Develop a sense of ease while working on your dreams. Make it a part of your life. If you don't get the message at first, you will probably dream it in another way. You don't need to work on every dream you write down, but it does help. Being consistent will create better results. If you aren't consistent, you begin to lose the ability to understand your dreams.

As you work with your dreams, your intuition improves and there is often an increase in the quality and quantity of information that you receive through your meditation practice.

One of the most interesting things about dreams is that they are written in a foreign language—the language of *symbol*s. As we work with dreams and learn the symbols, they seem to become a shorthand way of conveying information from our subconscious. In any case, the meaning of the symbol is personal to each of us.

When you look at the symbols within your dream, be careful not to depend on a dream symbol book. Remember that these symbols are *yours* and what the dream means is specific to *you*. No one can interpret the dream as well as you can. Other people can give you insights, but the true meaning can only come from you. On a deeper level you always know exactly what the dream means. We have enclosed a section at the end of the book for you to begin your personal symbol dictionary.

Journaling allows you to follow the pattern of your dreams, which is as important as the individual dream. Dreams work on many levels. When you do your dream work start with the physical level and move towards the spiritual. The journal can become very important in your life. It allows you to see the patterns that are developing in your subconscious.

Visions are waking dreams and usually bring us very powerful insights. Visions ordinarily come from the area of divine guidance and it is important to work with any visions that you have. Visions may reveal hidden promise. Working with dreams and visions is essential to your spiritual growth. Most of us don't have visions because there is too much going on in our minds during waking consciousness. When you have visions you need to realize that they are symbolic–like dreams are–and can't be looked at like ordinary reality. Sometimes visions appear during meditation and are there to give us extra information.

Daydreams are a related phenomenon, but are not as powerful as visions. Hallucinations come from the same source, but usually occur when a substance has broken down the barriers of normal consciousness—or a high fever can do the same thing.

The spiritual world is all around us. It exists simultaneously but operates at a faster frequency. There are many levels that exist within the spiritual world. One of these is the Akashic record—the history of the past and future (within probabilities). Sometimes during our sleep, we can intersect with the Akashic record and have warning precognitive dreams. Sometimes we won't remember the experience but the next day we may have flashes of what seems like ESP telling us things that are about to happen. There are also places in the spiritual world where there are great teachers or masters who can give us spiritual teachings. We may or may not remember this teaching experience, but it can change our waking life by the reactions we have. The more we work with our dreams, the more we integrate the parts of ourselves and bring our being into balance. Then we are more ready for higher teachings. This may come through dreams, meditation, insights, intuitions or hunches.

Chapter 6
Common Dream Themes

You are the one who really knows the meaning of your dreams. You created the dream, and the symbols personally key into your life. There are, however, some common themes that may run through many of your dreams.

RECURRING DREAMS

A recurring dream is often an indicator that change is coming into your life. The change is connected to a lesson that you are working on, but haven't completed yet. Often this type of dream shows that you haven't learned something or are missing a message for your life. A recurring dream always indicates special significance. You won't necessarily quit dreaming it when you come to understand the dream. You will need to finish the lesson to be done with the dream.

FALLING AND FLYING DREAMS

Both of these may indicate that your inner being is leaving the physical body while you are sleeping. Flying dreams can be enjoyable and it is possible to gain control of the experience and decide where you want to go. Falling dreams often indicate that you are coming back into the physical body too rapidly. On a symbolic level the confirmation of flying and falling often indicate moving into higher levels of consciousness and the need to stay there.

DEATH AND DYING DREAMS

These dreams rarely indicate physical death. More often they are talking about dying parts of the self. Old parts of you that are outgrowing may die symbolically in your dreams. These types of dreams can also show you that there are parts of you that are dead. These latter dreams indicate a need to awaken and become more sensitive. When you are being killed in your dreams, external factors are at work. You need to look at the rest of the dream to determine whether you are outgrowing old stuff or need more nurturing of the self.

RUNNING DREAMS

If you are running or being chased in your dreams, it may indicate that you are avoiding or running away from something in your life. These dreams are telling you to turn around and face whatever problems you are currently not facing.

NIGHTMARES

These dreams are really trying to get your attention. The subconscious pushes through our reality with a dream that shows us the out-of-balance places in our lives. Nightmares can be very effective teaching dreams. Not only do they get our attention, but we tend to remember them longer and are more inclined to work them out.

BATHROOM DREAMS

This type of dream shows us we are processing the issues of our lives. The dreams can be on physical, mental and emotional levels and indicate garbage that we are accumulating. Constipation may mean suppression. Diarrhea is the opposite but may also indicate that things are out of control. As a general theme, bathroom dreams show how we are dealing with issues from the past in order to live fully in the present.

Chapter 7
Dreamwork Techniques

This may be the most important section of the Dreamwork Book. We will be focusing on ways that you can decode and understand your dreams. There are, of course, many systems of doing this. We're going to focus on three. These techniques can be used singly or in combination to effectively work with your dreams.

SYMBOLS

One of the most interesting things about dreams is that they speak to us in symbols. At first, this may seem complicated, but as we learn to understand the meaning of symbols, our dreams become clearer. One of the reasons that dreams are given to us symbolically is that a symbol has a subjective, as well as an objective, meaning. It's more than the dictionary definition. Once we know our personal meaning of a symbol—we really know it. We feel it inside! Since we dream on more than one level, the symbols create a shorthand which helps us to decode the layers of meanings. There are also universal symbols which show up in our dreams and allow us to touch our spiritual selves. Dream symbols are part of our higher levels of consciousness.

Focusing on the symbols and learning to interpret them raises our consciousness. This element creates quantum leaps in awareness and consciousness.

At first, the process of interpreting symbols may seem awkward, but remember that you are learning a new skill. The more you practice, the better you will become.

If you choose to use a dream symbol dictionary, remember to use the definitions as a *guideline* rather than an absolute. Symbols often have more than one meaning and *your* meaning of the symbol may be different than the common one. The best symbol dictionary I have used is Betty Bethard's *The Dream Book*.

Begin in your dreamwork by acknowledging that on some level you already know the meaning of the dream—in fact you are the only one who does. On some level everything in the dream is you. All of the characters in the dream represent parts of yourself. They may either be showing you characteristics that you have or those you want. A vehicle, car, boat, plane or bicycle may represent your body and how it moves in your world. A house or building says things about yourself and how you are keeping order in the world. Water represents our emotions; the earth, our connection to the ground: and fences and roads, the blocks in our lives. Once you begin to recognize some basic symbols, the decoding becomes easier. Remember that your dream probably has more than one level involved in its meaning. Now, let's take a symbol like a house. Look at obvious meanings and associations ... see as well as feel. What does a house mean to you? Use the following page to write about the symbol of a house.

THE HOUSE

WORKING WITH SYMBOLS

Write the story of your dream.

Record symbols with their meaning—be sure to *personalize* the meaning.

Work on the interpretation.

DIALOGUING

In order to help you become familiar with this technique, try the following exercise:

Become quiet, calm and receptive. Ask your self, "If I was a house, what would I look like? I am a house ... what do I look like?" Observe the images and feelings, simply accept what you see and experience. Experience yourself as a house. Is there a yard? What does the interior look like? Feel like? Are there pets or people in the house? Don't be limited by what I say— let your imagination go free. What do you feel? Are you a happy house?

Now write down what this experience was like.

I AM THE HOUSE:

Circle the symbols within the symbol of the house.

Pick one of the symbols—the one you find the most interesting.

THE SYMBOL:________________________________

Close your eyes and speak to the symbol as if it were alive. Begin by saying, "I am the red chair." Now take the part of a second symbol and have it speak to you as if they were answering you. Have different symbols talk to each other. Simply allow this to take place. Free associate the conversation, letting your intuition guide you. This is a very powerful tool, so use it. When you feel complete with the experience, open your eyes and write about it.

WHAT THE SYMBOL SAYS:

WHAT THE SYMBOL MEANS:

WORKING WITH DIALOGUING

Write the story of the dream.

Record the symbols—dialogue with them.

Work on the interpretation.

ALCHEMY

Alchemical dreamwork is one of the techniques of Alchemical Hypnotherapy, which was developed by David Quigley in California during the mid 1980's. The alchemical process resolves conflicts within the self by connecting us to our Higher Self, which I choose to call our Inner Self. This allows for the highest levels of wholeness and creativity. The combination of humanistic and spiritual perspectives allows us to achieve meaningful changes. Alchemical dreamwork focuses on using the dream world to achieve these results. This "alchemy" creates transformation through the dream.

The work is done in a meditative or trance state. The intent is to reenter the dream and reexperience the dream for greater clarity and understanding.

It is possible to become the various elements in the dream—allowing you to find out what their real meaning is for your life.

Dreamwork Techniques

WORKING WITH ALCHEMY

1. Be clear about issues and goals.

2. Tell the dream story.

3. Identify the major feeling of the dreams.

4. Identify the dominant thought or thinking.

5. Reenter the dream. (Hypnotic or meditative trance)

6. Run the dream or the dream segment.

7. Dialogue with the dream figures.

8. Act out the dream story and become each symbol and/or person.

9. Expand the dream to see what you didn't see or feel before.

10. Pause the dream. Go back to the first time you felt this way in this lifetime. Look for connection to what's happening now.

11. Continue to completion. Go to the very end of the dream … beyond what you remember.

12. Return to normal consciousness, notice your feelings and thoughts. Write about your experience.

Dreams are very important in helping us gain a greater self-knowledge. They help you see yourself as you truly are. They can connect you with your beautiful Inner Self, your potential. They also show you what you are learning and what you are missing from your life. You do not need to suffer to grow. It can be an exciting experience to come to know yourself. When you dream of a particular problem or situation in your life, remember that the dream can help you to creatively resolve issues.

As you work with your dreams, you will begin to be aware when you are dreaming. When confronted with strange images, you can ask what they mean and get immediate information. Dreams are very effective tools to use for personal growth and development. By working with dreams, you will raise your awareness and gain greater intuition.

Dreams give us insight about our life lessons. Waking reality gives us a chance to practice those insights. To grow and change, we need to integrate the insights into our lives. On one level we create all our experiences in our lives to teach ourselves lessons. Our dreams can help us to understand the lessons better. Through your dream symbols, you will see the way your thought patterns work. By working with dreams you will move naturally into higher levels of consciousness and understanding which has the power to transform yourself and your life.

Chapter 8

DREAMWORK PROGRAM

This section is designed to teach you how to program and interpret dreams. There is space to record and work on dreams. We will use a cycle of five dreams. At the beginning of every cycle, decide your current issue. Program yourself each night to work on that issue. Use only one issue at a time and record the next five dreams that you remember. Work on the dream by telling the story, identifying key symbols, working on the interpretation and then determining an action or an affirmation that reinforces your work on the dream. When you complete a cycle of five dreams, determine what you have learned and what you need to do. Three different cycles are provided for you. It is easier than it sounds to work on three different issues. At the end of the cycle take a look at what you have learned and decide what you need to do next.

Step 1   Select Your Issue.

First, determine an issue in your life that you want to work on through your dreams. Issues come out of awareness of your present life. An issue is like a reactive complex– a set of behaviors, feelings and thoughts about a common problem. Behavior is motivated by feelings and validated by thoughts. Issues become triggered by threads of memories.

Step 2   Program your dreams to work on your issue.

Using the Dreamwork Tape is very effective.

Step 3   Write down the dream.

Do this as fully as you can ... give each dream a short title. This is the Dream Story.

Step 4   Identify the symbols.

Note the possible meaning beside them ... try the symbol exercise given or check a dream dictionary. Meanings will seldom be absolute, depending on what the meaning is to the dreamer.

Step 5   Write down the interpretation.

Use the meaning of the symbols, combined with the messages you get from dialoguing with the symbols, to "see" and "feel" what this dream means. Then, apply it to your life.

Step 6   Come up with an action or affirmation to create growth from what you learned.

Follow an issue through five dreams.

Step 7   Create positive change out of what you learn.

Dreamwork Program

My Issue

Dream Story

Dreamwork Program

Dream Story

43

Key
Symbols

45

Actions / Affirmations

Dream Story

Dream Story

Key
Symbols

Interpretation

Dreamwork Program

Actions / Affirmations

Dream Story

Dreamwork Program

Dream Story

53

Key
Symbols

Interpretation

Action / Affirmations

Dream Story

Dreamwork Program

Dream Story

58

Key
Symbols

Interpretation

Dreamwork Program

Action / Affirmations

Dream Story

Dreamwork Program

Dream Story

63

64

Interpretation

Action / Affirmation

Dreamwork Program

What I Learned or Need To Do

67

Dreamwork Program

What I Learned or Need To Do

68

The Dreamwork Book

Dreamwork Program

My Issue

Dream Story

Dreamwork Program

Dream Story

Key
Symbols

Interpretation

The Dreamwork Book

Action / Affirmations

Dream Story

Dream Story

76

Key
Symbols

Interpretation

Dreamwork Program

Action / Affirmations

Dream Story

Dreamwork Program

Dream Story

Key
Symbols

Interpretation

Action / Affirmation

Dream Story

Dream Story

86

Key
Symbols

Interpretation

Dreamwork Program

Action / Affirmations

Dream Story

Dreamwork Program

Dream Story

Key
Symbols

Interpretation

The Dreamwork Book

Action / Affirmations

Dreamwork Program

What I Learned or Need to Do

95

96

Dreamwork Program

My Issue

Dream Story

Dreamwork Program

Dream Story

Key
Symbols

Interpretation

Action / Affirmations

Dream Story

Dream Story

Key
Symbols

Interpretation

Dreamwork Program

Action / Affirmation

Dream Story

Dreamwork Program

Dream Story

Key
Symbols

Interpretation

Action / Affirmations

Dream Story

Dream Story

Key
Symbols

Interpretation

Dreamwork Program

Action / Affirmations

Dream Story

Dreamwork Program

Dream Story

119

Key
Symbols

Interpretation

The Dreamwork Book

Action / Affirmations

Dreamwork Program

What I Learned or Need to Do

123

Chapter 9

As you work with your dreams, you will notice that certain symbols keep reoccurring. This section is for you to keep a record of your personal symbols and what they mean to you.

Personal Symbol Dictionary

Personal Symbol Dictionary

Personal Symbol Dictionary

Personal Symbol Dictionary

Zoilita Grant MS CHT

Zoilita Grant graduated from U.C. Berkeley in 1971 with B.A.'s in Anthropology and Psychology. She spent the next five years in British Columbia working with therapy groups. After two years in the U.S. Army, in military intelligence, she became a YMCA director in El Paso, Texas. Zoilita was extremely successful in the position, writing over $350,000 in grants. This led to her being selected as Citizen of the Year in 1979.

During this period, she began working on a Masters in counseling, which she received from The University of Texas in 1979. From 1980 to 1983, she worked as director of a drug and alcohol program in Ohio. For the past ten years, she has had a private practice in Auburn, CA and Boulder, CO. Zoilita is also a Certified Alchemical Hypnotherapist and taught for the Alchemy Institute in Denver for 3 ½ years.

In addition, she teaches classes in spiritual development and is available for consultation in this area. Zoilita recently co-facilitated the John Bradshaw workshop. While working for the Alchemy Institute she was certified as an Instructor of Hypnosis by the State of Colorado and was an examiner for the American Council of Hypnotists Examiners.

Zoilita lives in Longmont, Colorado with her husband Rick, and their children, Mark, 18, and Beth, 15. Bob, 23 and Pat, 21, live out of state.

Zoilita and Rick are partners in a new business called **MASTERKEY** which produces and markets "TOOLS FOR TRANSFORMATION." These tools are tapes, books, manuals and classes designed to facilitate the transformation of consciousness.

Zoilita has been involved in the personal growth movement since the mid-1960's. She has done a personal Vision Quest and has had a meditative practice for about 26 years.

Suggested Reading List

Bethards, Betty, *The Dream Book: Symbols for Self-Understanding* (Inner Light Foundation, 1983)

Colton, Ann Ree, *Watch Your Dreams* (ARC Publishing Company, 1973)

Corriere, Richard, Werner Karle, Lee Woldenberg and Joseph Hart, *Dreaming & Waking* (Peace Press, 1980)

Gackenbach, Jayne, and Jane Bosveld, *Control Your Dreams* (Harper & Row, 1989)

Garfield, Patricia, *Creative Dreaming* (Ballantine Books, 1974)

Hobson, J. Allen, *The Dreaming Brain* (Basic Books, 1988)

Hopcke, Robert H., *Men's Dreams, Men's Healing* (Shambhala Publications, 1990)

Morris, Jill, *The Dream Workbook* (Ballantine Books, 1985)

Read, Henry, *Dream Solutions* (New World Library, 1991)

Sanford, John A., *Dreams and Healing* (Paulist Press, 1978)

Sechrist, Elsie, *Dreams: Your Magic Mirror* (Cowles Book Company, 1968)

Winski, Norman, *Understanding Jung* (Sherbourne Press, 1971)